D0055146

THE POETICS OF

ARISTOTLE

THE POETICS OF

ARISTOTLE

Translated by Preston H. Epps

CHAPEL HILL

The University of North Carolina Press

CONTENTS

	Preface	vii
I.	*Some Primary Facts and Principles*	1
II.	*Tragedy*	11
III.	*Epic Poetry*	49
IV.	*Criticisms of Poetry*	55
V.	*Epic and Tragedy Compared*	62
	Suggested Readings	65
	Literary Works Referred to in the Poetics	67
	Proper Names in the Poetics	69

PREFACE

1. Although it is hoped that there are some new elements in this translation and that it is in all cases correct, the primary aim in undertaking it was not to produce a "new" or a "corrected" translation of the *Poetics*. This will be clear to any reader acquainted with the standard translations. Nor was literary excellence the major consideration. A translation of the *Poetics*, to which all students could have simultaneous access and thus gain a common terminology for this work, has for some time been a desideratum for the course in Greek Drama. This translation is an effort to fill that need, and is, therefore, among other things, an attempt to make available a translation which an average student with reasonable industry can hope to understand without having to consult too many "aids and explanations." A clear statement of what, according to the Oxford Classical Text, Aristotle said, has been the chief concern, and whatever seemed likely to contribute to that end has been welcomed.

2. The writer of the *Poetics* was apparently too steeped in the background of Greek literature and poetry to feel the necessity of making his statements as full and complete as they should be. As a result, we have in the *Poetics* "a mode of statement often elliptical, allusive, and overcharged with meaning . . . which . . . frequently omits to indicate the connection of ideas in the sentences and paragraphs, so that the logical relation between them is

left for us to perceive as best we can." [1] It has seemed
necessary, therefore, to add words and at times phrases
to make explicit what seemed clearly implicit—a danger-
ous, though in this case, it is hoped, not an abused practice.

3. A rigid effort has been made to enclose in brackets
all instances of these "added" elements which seemed to
have any possibility of changing Aristotle's meaning in
any important way. Such as seemed only to round out
the sentence with a bit more clarity have not been enclosed in brackets but have been left unindicated. An
example of each type can be seen within the first two
pages of the translation. The first three words: "In this
treatise," are not in Aristotle's text. But to add these three
words did not seem to change Aristotle's meaning in any
important way. They were, therefore, not enclosed in
brackets. But on page 2 Aristotle is clearly contrasting
two procedures followed by two different types of artists. One artist is guided in making his imitation by rules
of art, while the other is guided by habit and practice
without reference to rules of art. To accentuate Aristotle's contrast here, I have added the word "mere" and
enclosed it in brackets; for it is possible that some inter-
preter might single this word out for special emphasis.
Interpreters should thus be spared the embarrassment and
confusion of emphasizing something which is not even in
Aristotle's text. These two examples will illustrate the
policy followed in this translation in regard to these
"added" elements. It is hoped that every addition which
might lead to any real difference in interpretation has
been enclosed in brackets.

4. Numerals and letters enclosed in parentheses have

[1] Ingram Bywater, ed., *Aristotle on the Art of Poetry* (Oxford,
1909), Preface, p. v.

been added as an aid to clarity. All other parentheses denote parentheses in the text of the *Poetics*. I have divided
the translation into five sections, indicated by Roman numerals. The arabic numbers indicate chapter divisions in
the text of the *Poetics*.

5. This translation has been made on the assumption
that translating is a question of transferring ideas rather
than word-meanings. The problem is to transfer the ideas
as completely as possible from one language into the other,
without loss or addition, in such a way that what is perceived and felt through the language of the translation is
as nearly as possible exactly what was perceived and felt
by those reading in the "original." This involves (1)
seeing just what is said in the original text and then (2)
stating this, not just in verbal equivalents of the words
used in the original *but in that vocabulary and idiom
through which the second language expresses what was
said in the original language*. This is what has been striven
for in the present translation.

6. No attempt has been made to arrive at a text for the
Poetics. The primary sources for a text are meagre indeed. The more conservative text arrived at by Vahlen
(1874), Christ (1878), Butcher (1898 and 1920), Bywater (1911) and Fyfe (1927) has been challenged by
Margoliouth (1911), by Rostagni (1927) and more re-
cently and vigorously by Gudeman (1934). Professor
Allan H. Gilbert, in his *Literary Criticism from Plato to
Dryden* (1938) has given us, with some omissions, a
translation of the *Poetics* based on Gudeman's text. The
differences among these editors seem to grow out of their
disagreement as to the place of importance to be assigned
to the two oldest extant codices, Parasinus 1761 (tenth
century) and Riccardianus 46 (fourteenth century),
along with the importance to be given to the Arabic

translation of the tenth or eleventh century. This Arabic translation is based on a Syriac translation of what is believed to be a fifth- or sixth-century Greek manuscript. This means that the Arabic translation is three removes from the original.

7. The problems raised by these two different approaches are complicated, and are such as demand experts for their final solution. A comparison of the Bywater (1911) and Gudeman (1934) texts shows some 280 variant readings, not counting such changes as the addition or omission of an article and changes in word order. Of these 280 changes made by Gudeman seventeen seem to involve noteworthy differences, while 173 fall into the following categories: (1) those which merely make the syntax smoother without any real difference in meaning; (2) those which do little more than make a text like Bywater's, for instance, more explicit; and (3) those which merely improve the literal accuracy. Of the remaining different readings in Gudeman's text, twenty-six are bracketed by him and ten are lacunae.

8. The present translation is based upon the more conservative text by Professor Ingram Bywater (1911)[2] in the Oxford Classical Texts series. This text was followed because it seemed as well-founded and as generally correct as any text can at present be known to be. Wherever another text has been followed that fact has been indicated by a footnote. Lacunae in Bywater's text have been indicated in this translation by asterisks in parentheses (****). The more crucial words of the text and those whose meaning is debated have been checked with the new Liddell & Scott lexicon.

---

[2] His readings which are bracketed as uncertain have been omitted in cases where they seemed unnecessary or to add nothing essential to the meaning of the sentence.

9. One can hardly hope to produce an errorless translation. It is hoped, however, that real errors in the meaning of the text have been kept at such a minimum that the serviceableness of the translation will not be seriously impaired by them.

10. It should always be understood without its having to be mentioned that but for the labors of editors and translators who have given their lives to a study of the *Poetics* this translation could never have been made, although they are not to be held responsible for any mistakes or shortcomings it may have. In crucial and obscure passages the first draft of this translation was compared with those of Butcher, Cooper, Bywater, and Fyfe (in the Loeb edition). Margoliouth's translation was discarded as useless after reading a few pages. Suggestions and helps from colleagues also have helped in many rough places. But of special help has been the very great kindness of Dr. Helmut Kuhn of our own Department of Philosophy and of Dr. Charles C. Mierow of Carleton College. Their service has been the greater because they each first read the translation through as an English essay and then read it through again in conjunction with the Greek text. Both made many valuable suggestions by which this translation has gained much in clarity and accuracy. This very great favor on the part of Dr. Kuhn and Dr. Mierow is most gratefully acknowledged, while they are at the same time absolved of all responsibility for any shortcomings the translation may still have.

11. One suggestion to the reader. Although the *Poetics* is attributed to one of the world's greatest philosophers and although it contains some definite Aristotelean philosophical ideas, it does not seem to be a philosophical work in purpose. In this work we have Aristotle the critic and analyzer rather than Aristotle the philosopher. The *Poetics*

will be better understood, therefore, and more appro-
priable if it is read and thought of as the analysis and
judgment of a keen mind trying to reduce a mass of
Greek poetic material to some intelligible order so that
its nature and forms could be better understood. The
work contains very penetrating insights; but if one will
observe as one reads, it will be found that wherever Aristotle happens to explain his statements they do not turn
out to be abstruse or obscure, but simple, straightforward,
rather evident and objective judgments. It is his com-
pressed and abbreviated style, plus the statements he does
not explain, which makes this work as difficult to understand as it is. As stated earlier, the aim of this translation
has been to put before the reader in clear English what,
according to Bywater's text, Aristotle actually said rather
than what Aristotle may have meant by what he said.
If this has been achieved, then the purpose which evoked
this translation has been realized.

P. H. Epps

The University of North Carolina
March 2, 1942

THE POETICS OF
ARISTOTLE

I

SOME PRIMARY FACTS

AND PRINCIPLES

1

In this treatise we propose to discuss (1) poetry itself; (2) the various forms it can take; (3) the function and potential possibilities of each form; (4) how the incidents of the plot must be arranged if the poem is to be a good one; (5) the number and kinds of parts various types of poetry may have; and (6) whatever else pertains to the same inquiry.[1] Let us begin, as is natural, with primary matters first.

Epic poetry, tragedy, and even comedy and the dithyramb, as well as most of the music written for the aulos [2] and the lyre, are all, taken as a whole, imitations.[3] Yet

Imitation, an integrating principle

---

[1] For numerals in parentheses see Preface, paragraph 4.

[2] The aulos is a Greek wood-wind instrument, most frequently referred to as a flute. But the evidence indicates that it was a reed instrument, and perhaps more like our clarinet or oboe.

[3] What Aristotle here means by imitation seems to be a portrayal of men as they (1) actively carry out some plan, purpose or design, or (2) as they go through some experience apart from action. See his remark on dancing near the end of this paragraph and also the first sentence of the first paragraph in chapter 2, *infra*. For a fuller treatment of the subject see Professor McKeon's article, "Literary Criticism and the Concept of Imitation in Antiquity," *Modern Philology*, XXXIV (1936), pp. 1-35.

they differ from each other in three respects: they imitate different things, in different ways, through different
means. For just as artists make imitations by means of
colors and figures (some in accordance with principles of
art and some in accordance with [mere] [4] habit and practice), while still others achieve their imitation through the
human voice, just so are imitations variously produced in
the case of the arts just mentioned. They all use language,
rhythm, and melody; but they use these either singly or
simultaneously. For instance, music for the aulos and lyre
uses only melody and rhythm, as do other types which
happen to have similar potential possibilities, such as music
for Panpipes. But the art of dancing uses rhythm without
any music; for in dancing, imitation of character, emotional experiences, and action are achieved through rhythm
accompanied by gestures. There is also a type of imitation
which uses nothing but language, either plain prose or
metrically arranged language, which is at times in one
kind of metre or again in several intermingled metres.
This type has never received a name; for we do not have
a common term which would comprise both the Socratic
dialogues and the mimes of Sophron and Xenarchus, not
even if they should be written in trimetric, elegiac, or
other such metres.

Yet men commonly call a writer a poet according to
whether he uses metre or not, rather than according to
the imitation he achieves. This is shown by the fact that
the Greek words for "elegiac" and "epic poet" are arrived
at by adding the word "poet" to the name of the metre used.
Then, too, if anyone produces in metre a treatise on medicine or natural philosophy, it is customary to speak of
him as a poet. Yet Homer and Empedocles have nothing

[4] See Preface, paragraph 3.

in common except the metre. Therefore, Homer should
be called a poet, while Empedocles should be called a
natural philosopher rather than a poet. Equally also would
a writer be called a poet if he should make his imitation
by intermingling all the metres, as has been done in
Chaeremon's *Centaur*, which is a poem for recitation made
up of all metres. So much, then, for these general matters.

But certain kinds of poetry employ all the above-men- *Means of*
tioned elements: rhythm, music, and metre. This is true *imitation*
of dithyrambic and of nomic poetry as well as of tragedy
and comedy. Yet these differ from each other in that
dithyrambic and nomic poetry use all three elements simultaneously while in tragedy and comedy they are used
separately at intervals. These, then, I call differences in
the artistic media through which men achieve imitation
in poetry.

2

Furthermore, since those who imitate choose as objects *Manner of*
of imitation men in action and since those in action must *portraying*
be either good or bad characters (inasmuch as character *objects*
almost always falls into one of these two categories ow-
ing to the fact that distinctions in human character are
all derived from the distinction between badness and good-
ness), they portray their characters as either better, or
worse, or such as we are. Painters follow the same practice. Polygnotus portrays them as better than we are,
Pauson as worse than we are, and Dionysius as we are. It
is evident, then, that each of the imitations mentioned will
exhibit these differences, and each will be different in pro-
portion as it imitates different objects in this threefold
way. These differences in portrayal can be achieved also
in dancing, and in aulos and lyre playing, as well as in

prose and in mere poetry without any music. For instance, Homer portrays men as better than we are, Cleophon as we are, and Hegemon of Thasos, the first to write burlesques, and Nicochares, who wrote the *Deliad*, as worse than we are. A similar portrayal can be achieved in dithyrambic and in nomic poetry, just as (****) [5] Timotheus and Philoxenus have done in their *Cyclops*. It is this difference in portrayal of character which distinguishes tragedy from comedy; for comedy strives to portray men as worse and tragedy as better than men now are.

3

Ways of presenting an imitation   There is a third difference in imitative portrayal: how the imitation shall in each case be presented. For it is possible to present an imitation of the same object through the same medium in one of three ways: (1) one may tell the story, now directly in person and now through some assumed character, as Homer does; or (2) one may set forth the entire imitation without any change in person; or (3) one may have the characters being portrayed execute the entire imitation. Imitations, then, just as was said in the beginning, differ from each other in three respects: in the objects imitated; in the means used; and in the manner of presentation.

Origin of words tragedy and comedy   As an imitative artist, then, Sophocles would be like Homer in that each portrays good men, but also like Aristophanes in that both he and Aristophanes portray men in action and doing things. Indeed, some claim that drama took its name from the fact that it imitated men as they were doing [*dra*-ontas] things. From this etymological

―――――――――――――――

[5] See Preface, paragraph 8.

argument the Dorians [6] contend that both tragedy and comedy originated among them—the Megarians in Megara and Sicily claiming comedy as their invention, and some of the Peloponnesians insisting that tragedy was theirs. The Megarians assert that comedy originated in Megara during the time of the democracy while those in Sicily contend that it originated with them, since Epicharmus was their citizen and lived much earlier than Chionides and Magnes.[7] These Dorians appeal to the words "comedy" and "tragedy" as proof of their contention. They observe that they call their surrounding districts *comae* while the Athenians call theirs *demoi*, and that the word for comic actors [*comodoi*], is derived not from *comad-sein*, meaning "to revel," but from the fact that these actors, being expelled from cities as unworthy of recognition, wandered from *comae* to *comae* [and thus came to be called *comodoi*]. They assert further that the Dorian word for action is *dra*-n while the Athenian word for action is *pratt*-ein. So much, then, for the differences in imitation, both as to the number of these differences and what they are.

4

Two causes, and natural ones too, seem generally responsible for the rise of the art of poetry: (1) the natural desire to imitate, which is present from childhood and differentiates man as the most imitative of all living crea-

The matrix of poetry

---

[6] The two largest ethnical divisions of the Greeks were Ionians and Dorians. The peoples of Megara, the greater part of the Peloponnesus and of Sicily are thought to have been largely Dorians.

[7] Epicharmus, Chionides, and Magnes are said to be early writers of comedy.

tures as well as enables him to gain his earliest knowledge through imitation, and (2) universal enjoyment in imitations. We find an indication of this in experience: for we view with pleasure reproductions of objects which in real life it pains us to look upon—likenesses of very loathsome animals or dead bodies, for instance. This is especially true if the reproductions are executed with unusual accuracy. The reason for this is that learning is the most pleasant of all experiences, not only for philosophers but for the rest of mankind as well, although mankind has but a small share in this experience. In fact, mankind's pleasure in beholding likenesses of objects is due to this: as they contemplate reproductions of objects they find themselves gaining knowledge as they try to reason out what each thing is; for instance, that this man is such and such a person. Of course, if the spectator happens never to have seen the object which is depicted, the pleasure he experiences will not be due to the reproduction as such, but to the workmanship, or the color, or some similar reason.

Elements in the development of drama   Now since man is by nature inclined toward imitation, melody, and rhythm (for the metres of poets evidently stem from rhythm), man had these propensities to begin with, and it was by developing them little by little that *Improvisations* poetry was finally created from improvisations. The next step was a gradual division of poetry according to the inherent characters of the poets. The nobler poets portrayed *Two kinds of poets* noble deeds and deeds of noble individuals, while the cheaper ones portrayed the deeds of cheap persons, writing malevolent satires at first, just as the nobler poets at first wrote hymns and encomia. It is true that we have no example of malevolent satire prior to Homer, though it is likely that many existed. But, from Homer on, we do have examples such as his *Margites* [8] and the like. Iambic very fittingly became the metre used in these malevolent satires; for it is even now called iambic because it is in that metre that men lampoon each other. There were at first, then, two classes of ancient poets: those who used heroic and those who used iambic verse.

Moreover, just as Homer was the poet par excellence of the serious and noble, since he was the only one who wrote not only excellent poetic imitations but dramatic ones too, so also was he the first to give us the general outlines of comedy by giving us dramatic imitations of the humorous rather than of malevolent satire. For the *Margites* contains as definite analogues for comedy as the *Iliad* and the *Odyssey* do for tragedy. And so, when tragedy and comedy came into being, poets turned to one or the other of these, each according as his particular type of character urged him; and those who had in earlier times become poets of malevolent satire then became comic poets, and those who for a similar reason earlier became epic poets then became writers of tragedy; for tragedy and comedy were at that time regarded as greater and more esteemed than epic poetry and malevolent satire. *Analogues for tragedy and comedy*

To take up the question of whether or not tragedy is already sufficiently developed in regard to its formal parts, and to come to a conclusion on the basis of the question itself and of its relation to the theatre would require another discussion. We do know, however, that both tragedy and comedy grew out of improvisations, tragedy eventuating from the improvisations of composer-leaders of dithyrambs and comedy from those of composer-leaders of phallic song rites which survive as customs in many *Dithyramb and phallic rites*

[8] Aristotle thought that Homer wrote the *Margites*, but it is now known to be by someone else. Consequently, his ensuing argument that the *Margites* proves that Homer gave the Greeks the general principles of comedy is not valid.

cities even until today. Writers gradually added to these improvisations as they developed each newly discovered element of drama, and, after going through many changes, tragedy ceased to develop when it had achieved its natural growth.

Aeschylus   The number of actors was first raised from one to two by Aeschylus. He also reduced the choral element in tragedy and started the spoken [as opposed to the choral] part on its way to becoming the most important part of *Sophocles* tragedy. Sophocles increased the number of actors to three, and introduced painted scenery. As to its greatness and loftiness, tragedy was late in arriving at an august character because (1) it had to grow out of its satyric form, as well as (2) outgrow its slender plots and (3) its *Metres* uncouth language. Its metre was changed from trochaic tetrameter to iambic trimeter; for tragedy used trochaic tetrameter at first on account of its being satyric poetry and more concerned with dancing. But when a spoken part was added to tragedy, nature herself discovered the proper metre for it; for of all metres iambic is the one best suited to spoken parts. This is shown by the fact that in ordinary conversation we use iambics frequently but seldom use a hexameter, and even then we have to depart from the intonation of ordinary conversation. There was also [an increase in] the number of episodes. As to the other details of tragedy and how they are said to have reached their present orderly arrangement, let what has been said be considered sufficient; for it would doubtless be quite a task to explain each of these matters in detail.

5

Early comedy   Comedy is, as we have said, an imitation of cheaper, more ordinary persons. They are not entirely base, but

are embodiments of that part of the ugly which excites
laughter. Now the part of the ugly which excites laughter
is that which has some flaw or ugliness which causes neither pain nor harm, just as an ugly and distorted mask
immediately brings laughter but causes no pain. The
changes tragedy went through and the media through
which these changes were effected are pretty well known.
But the early history of comedy is not known because
comedy did not at first receive serious consideration. This
is natural since early comedy was presented by volunteer
actors, and it was not until late that the archon first
granted a chorus to writers of comedy.[9] The so-called
early comic writers speak of comedy as having already
acquired certain forms; but no one knows (1) who introduced comic masks or (2) who introduced prologues,
(3) who increased the number of actors from time to
time, and (4) other similar details. The making of comic
plots began in Sicily (****) with Epicharmus and Phormis. At Athens, Crates was the first comic writer to aban-
don lampooning [as the chief end of comedy] and gen-
eralize the plot and subject matter.

Epic poetry and tragedy are alike in that they are both *Elements com-*
imitations of noble characters and use stately metres; but *mon to epic*
they differ in that epic poetry is narrative and uses only *and tragedy*
one metre [while tragedy uses several]. They differ also
in the time consumed by the events treated, although epic
and tragedy were originally alike in this respect; for tragedy [now] tries as far as possible to limit the time of its
action to one revolution of the sun or to depart only
slightly from that rule, but epic poetry does not so limit
itself in time. Of their essential elements, some are the

---

[9] I.e., officially recognized it. The date when a chorus was first
granted to a writer of comedy is generally said to be 487/6 B.C.

same, and some are peculiar to tragedy. Therefore, whoever knows what constitutes good and bad tragedy knows also what constitutes good and bad epic; for tragedy has all the essential elements of epic poetry, but epic poetry does not have all the elements essential to tragedy.

II

TRAGEDY

6

We will speak later about imitation in epic poetry and about comedy.[1] Let us now resume our discussion of tragedy by deducing the definition of its essential nature which follows from what we have said.

Tragedy, then, is an imitation, through action rather *Definition* than narration, of a serious, complete, and ample action, by means of language rendered pleasant at different places in the constituent parts by each of the aids [used to make language more delightful], in which imitation there is also effected through pity and fear its catharsis [2] of these and similar emotions.

---

[1] Aristotle's discussion of comedy has not survived, if it was ever written. He may have discussed it in the "lost" second book of the *Poetics*. There is some evidence that such a book was written.

[2] No word used by Aristotle has caused more debate than this one, and readers will find many translations and explanations of it. One should begin one's reading in explanation of it with Bywater's lengthy note, and then read in other commentaries. Some notion of the controversy precipitated by the use of this word in this definition may be gained by consulting D. W. Robertson, Jr., "A Preliminary Survey of the Controversy over Aristotle's Doctrine of Tragic Catharsis" (1937). A University of North Carolina Master's dissertation.

By "language rendered pleasant" I mean language which has rhythm, [instrumental] melody, and song. By "aids at different places" I mean that some parts use metre alone while in other parts the language is aided by song. Since the imitation in tragedy is achieved through action, the orderly arrangement of what appeals to the eye must first of all necessarily be an essential part of tragedy. After this would come music and diction, since it is through these that the imitation is effected. By "diction" here I mean the metrical arrangement. What is meant by "music" is entirely obvious.

Now tragedy is an imitation of an action being carried out by certain individuals who must be certain kinds of persons in character and in thinking [3]—the two criteria by which we determine the quality of an action; for character and one's thinking are two natural causes of action, and it is because of these that all men fail or succeed. The plot is the imitation of the action to be presented. I here mean by "plot" the arrangement of the incidents. By

[3] The Greek word here (*dianoia*) is the second of the three most difficult words in the *Poetics* to translate. The number of times (four) Aristotle takes pains to explain its meaning seems to indicate that he too sensed a difficulty in its use here. The new Liddell & Scott Greek lexicon lists (with references) five meanings for the word: (1) "thought, i.e., intention, purpose"; (2) "process of thinking"; (3) "thinking faculty, understanding"; (4) "thought expressed, meaning of a word or passage"; and (5) "intellectual capacity revealed in speech or action by characters in the drama." This lexicon cites the passages in the *Poetics* as its basis for this fifth meaning.

But an examination of Aristotle's four explanations in the *Poetics* makes it seem that he had in mind in his use of this word: (1) intellectual deliberative capacity; (2) the process of thinking; and (3) the thoughts one gives assent to and acts upon. The variations in translation for this word found herein represent an effort to suggest to the reader the various meanings this word *seems* to have in the *Poetics*. They are not offered as entirely satisfactory translations but as the best means the translator could hit upon for the different meanings Aristotle *seems* to have intended.

"character" I mean that by which we determine what kinds of men are being presented; and by "one's thinking" I mean that which manifests itself in all the characters say when they present an argument or even make evident an opinion. Therefore, every tragedy must necessarily have six elements according to which the quality of the tragedy is determined: [4] (1) plot, (2) character [indicants], (3) thought, (4) spectacle, (5) diction, and (6) music. We thus have three parts (1, 2, 3) which tell us what the tragedy proposes to achieve an imitation of, one (4) which tells us how it proposes to do so, and two (5 & 6) which tell us the means to be used. These constitute all the parts. Therefore, just about all the dramatists use these constituent forms—which is very natural since every drama equally admits of spectacle, character [indicants], plot, diction, music, and thought. *Constituent elements*

But the most important of these is the arrangement of the incidents of the plot; for tragedy is not the portrayal of men [as such], but of action, of life.[5] Happiness and misery are the result of action, and the end [of life(?)] is a certain kind of action and not a quality. Men are the certain kinds of individuals they are as a result of their character; but they become happy or miserable as a result of their actions. Consequently, dramatists do not employ action in order to achieve character portrayal, but they include character because of its relation to action. Therefore, the incidents and plot constitute the end of tragedy, and the end is the greatest thing of all. Moreover, without action there could be no tragedy, but there could be *Plot*

---

[4] I.e., whether simple, complex, tragedy of character, spectacle, etc.

[5] Bywater's text has a lacuna here and is otherwise so confused that I have here followed Gudeman in (1) putting a period after "life" and (2) in using his text as a basis for the sentence immediately following.

tragedy without character. In fact, most of the new tragedies are without character. Speaking generally, there are many portrayers of imitations of which the same is true, as is seen in the case of the painters Zeuxis and Polygnotus. Polygnotus' works contain excellent portrayals of character, but there is no character portrayal in a painting of Zeuxis. Furthermore, if anyone should arrange in proper order a number of speeches which showed moral character and were well written from the point of view of diction and the thought [of those represented], he would not achieve the end of tragedy. This end would be much better achieved by a tragedy which was inferior in these elements, yet had a plot and arrangement of incidents. Moreover, the two most compelling elements in tragedy—reversals and recognitions—are parts of the plot. A further proof is the fact that even those who undertake to write tragedy can become proficient in matters of diction and character [indicants] sooner than they can in arranging the incidents of the plot, as is proved by almost all the earlier poets. Therefore, the first principle and, as it were, the soul of tragedy is the plot.

Character   The second is the character [indicants]. It is the same also in painting; for if anyone should make a painting by smearing the most beautiful colors at random on a surface his painting would not give as much pleasure as a [mere] figure done in outline. Tragedy is an imitation of action, and is for that reason principally concerned with characters in action.

Thought   The third part is the thinking ability of the characters, which is the ability to [think out and] say (1) what is possible [within the limits of the situation] and (2) what is fitting—a function which is the same as that of language when used in statesmanship and in oratory. Thus it happens that the early poets had their characters speak like statesmen, but contemporary ones have theirs speak like rhetoricians.

Character [indicants] are those elements which make clear, in matters where it is not otherwise evident, a person's choice—what sorts of things he chooses or avoids. Therefore, speeches in which a character is in no way confronted with something he must choose or reject, do not have character [indicants].

Thought manifests itself in what the characters say as they prove or disprove something or make evident something universal.

The fourth thing in our list is diction, and by "diction" *Diction* I mean, just as we stated earlier, expression [of thought] by means of language—a power which is the same in both metrical and non-metrical language.

Of the remaining elements, music has the greatest enriching power; and spectacle, while quite appealing, is the most inartistic and has the least affinity with poetry; for the essential power of tragedy does not depend upon the presentation and the actors. Moreover, for achieving the effects of spectacle, the art of the mechanic of stage properties is more competent than the art of poetry.

7

Since these matters have been defined, let us discuss *Arrangement* next the kind of arrangement of incidents a tragedy must *of plot* have, since this is the most primary and important essential of tragedy. We have laid it down that tragedy is an imitation of an action which is whole, complete, and of a certain magnitude. Now it is possible to have a whole which does not have magnitude. A whole is that which has a beginning, a middle, and an end. A beginning is that which of necessity does not follow anything, while something by nature follows or results from it. On the other hand, an end is that which naturally, of necessity, or most generally follows something else but nothing follows it. A middle is that which follows and is followed by something. Therefore, those who would arrange plots well must not begin just anywhere in the story nor end at just any point, but they must adhere to the criteria here laid down.

Proper Furthermore, everything beautiful, both animate and
magnitude those inanimate things which have been created from certain parts, must have not only the arrangement just described, but must have also a proper magnitude; for beauty consists in magnitude and arrangement. And so, a very small animal could not be beautiful, because our perception of it, taking place at close range and in an imperceptible amount of time, is confused. Nor could a very large animal, one a thousand miles long, for instance, be beautiful to us, because we cannot see it all at once and perception of it as a unity and a whole eludes us. Therefore, just as there must be a proper magnitude in the case of animate and created inanimate things—a magnitude which can be easily taken in as a whole by the eye—so must plots have a proper length—one which can be easily retained within the memory.

Time limit The limit which dramatic contests and the perceptive powers [of an audience] impose upon the length of a tragedy is not a part of the art of poetry; for if it had been the rule to enter a hundred tragedies [6] in the "tragic" contests, the time for each would have been limited by the water clock, as it is said was once the case in some places. The length-limit dictated by the very nature of the thing is always this: the greater the limit, provided the

---

[6] I.e., instead of the nine or twelve which were entered.

whole continues readily comprehensible, the more beautiful it will be because of its magnitude. And so, a general
definition of magnitude for an action would be: that
amount of magnitude in which events proceeding in suc-
cession according to probability and necessity veer around
from bad to good fortune or from good to bad. This is
a sufficient delimitation for magnitude.

8

Some people think a plot can be said to be a unified *Unity of plot*
one if it merely centers about one person. But this is not
true; for countless things happen to that one person some
of which in no way constitute a unit. In just the same
way there are many actions of an individual which do not
constitute a single action. Therefore, those poets who
write a Heracleid, a Thesiad, and poems of that kind appear to be following a wrong principle; for they think
that since Heracles was a single individual any plot dealing with him must of necessity have unity. But Homer,
just as he excels in other matters, seems, either through
natural insight or art, to have been right in this also; for
in composing an *Odyssey* he did not include an account
of everything which happened to Odysseus. He omitted
his being struck by a boar on Parnassus,[7] for instance, and

---

[7] Commentators seem fond of pointing out that Aristotle is here
in error. The fact is that the scar is used four times in the *Odyssey*
to identify Odysseus. In the first instance (*Od.* 19:386-466) the
story is told in full. In the other places (21:217-20; 23:73-74; and
24:331-32) it is merely mentioned by some one or is displayed by
Odysseus. If Aristotle had in mind one of the last three passages
his statement is correct. If he meant that the story is nowhere told
in full in the *Odyssey*, the statement is incorrect, on the basis of
our present text. It is possible, however, that Aristotle had a text
different from ours. And it is possible that his memory let him
down.

his feigned madness when the Greeks were assembling for Troy, because neither of these by having happened made probable or inevitable some other incident. But Homer has made both the *Iliad* and the *Odyssey* centre around an action which is unified in the sense we are demanding. Therefore, just as in other mimetic arts a unified imitation is an imitation of a single thing, in the same way the plot in tragedy, since it is an imitation of an action, must deal with that action and with the whole of it; and the different parts of the action must be so related to each other that if any part is changed or taken away the whole will be altered and disturbed. For anything whose presence or absence makes no discernible difference is no essential part of the whole.

9

Poet and historian   It is evident also, from what has been said, that it is not the function of the poet to relate what has happened but what can happen according to the law of probability or necessity. Whether the writer is a historian or a poet is not to be determined by whether he uses metre or prose; for the writings of Herodotus could be put into metre and still be history just as completely with metre as without it. The difference between a poet and a historian is this: the historian relates what has happened, the poet what could happen. Therefore, poetry is something more philosophic and of more serious import than history; for poetry tends to deal with the general, while history is concerned with delimited particular facts. An instance of "the general" [with which poetry undertakes to deal] is this: what are the sorts of things which, according to the law of probability and necessity, various types of individuals tend to do and say? This is what poetry aims to make evident when it attaches names to characters. An instance of "particular facts" [with which history deals] is: what did Alcibiades do, or what was done to him?

In [present-day] comedy [8] this [using of names to indi- *Names in drama* cate types] has already become evident; for when writers of comedy have constructed their plots from what is probable, they add any names they care to, and do not write about particular individuals as iambic poets do. But tragedy holds on to its traditionally established names, for the reason that men tend to believe what has been proved possible. We tend to believe that what has not yet happened is not yet possible; but what has happened is evidently possible, since it would not have happened if it had not been possible. Yet in some tragedies there are only one or two traditionally familiar names and the rest are invented, while in others, Agathon's *Antheus*, for instance, there are no familiar names, but everything, both names and incidents, are the author's invention. And yet they give just as much pleasure. Therefore, tragic poets should not insist upon holding on, without exception, to the traditional plots around which tragedies are generally constructed. This would be ridiculous, since the familiar plots, though familiar to only a few, delight everybody. From these facts it is evident, therefore, that the tragic poet must be rather a "maker" of plots than of metrical lines,[9] since (1) he is a tragic poet by virtue of the imitation he achieves, and (2) it is action which he gives an imitation of. Nor is he any less a tragic poet if he happens to portray events which have already happened; for certainly some of the things which have happened are such

[8] I.e., late Greek comedy in Aristotle's day (384–322 B.C.) up until the time the *Poetics* was written (perhaps about 330 B.C.).

[9] It is well to keep in mind as one reads the *Poetics* that the Greek word for poet means literally "maker."

as would be probable and possible, which is the law the poet follows in making an imitation of them.

Types of plot   Of simple plots and actions, the episodic are the worst. By an "episodic plot" I mean one in which the episodes are not arranged according to the law of probability and *Episodic* necessity. Poor poets make such plots because of their poor ability; good poets make them on account of the actors; [10] for since they are writing works for competition and have stretched out the plot beyond its natural possibilities, they are frequently compelled to distort natural sequence. But tragedies are imitations not only of actions which are complete but of such as inspire pity and fear; and actions tend to inspire most pity and fear whenever (1) they happen contrary to expectation and (2) are brought about one by the other. For anything so brought about will appear more wonderful than if it happens spontaneously or by chance, since, of the things which happen by chance, those seem to excite more wonder which appear to have happened in accordance with some design, such as when the statue of Mitys in Argos fell on the murderer of Mitys and killed him as he was witnessing a festival.* Such things seem to happen according to some design. Therefore, this type of plot must necessarily be the best.

10

Simple and   There are two types of plot: the simple and the com-
complex   plex. This is natural since actions, too, are simple and complex, and plots are imitations of actions. By a "simple action" I mean one which is single and continuous, as de-

---

[10] Gudeman's text has "judges."
* The expression here translated "as he was witnessing a festival" can also mean "while he was looking at the statue." The Greek is ambiguous.

fined above, whose change of fortune comes about without a reversal or recognition scene. By a "complex" action I mean one whose change of fortune is brought about by a reversal or a recognition scene, or both.[11] These [reversals and recognitions] must grow out of the arrangement of the plot itself by its being so constructed that each succeeding incident happens necessarily or according to probability from what has happened previously; for it makes a great deal of difference whether the incidents happen because of what has preceded or merely after it.

11

A reversal is a change of the type described above [12] by *Reversal* which the action veers around in the opposite direction, and that, too, as we said, in accordance with the laws of probability or necessity, just as, in the *Oedipus Tyrannus*, the servant who comes to cheer Oedipus and free him of his fear of his mother by telling him who he is, does just the opposite. So, too, in the *Lynceus* the hero is being led away to death and Danaus is following along to do the killing, but it turns out from what has happened that Danaus is killed and the hero is saved.

As the name makes clear, recognition is a change by *Recognition* which those marked [by the plot] for good or for bad fortune pass from a state of ignorance into a state of knowledge which disposes them either to friendship or enmity towards each other. The best type of recognition is one which is accompanied by reversal, such as happens in the *Oedipus Tyrannus*. There are, of course, recogni-

[11] The terms "reversal" and "recognition" are explained in the following paragraphs.
[12] The last sentence in chapter 10, immediately above.

tions of other things also. As we have defined the term, there could be recognition with reference to inanimate things or to things of ordinary every-day life. There could also be recognition of whether some one has or has not done something. But the recognition especially related to plot and action is the one defined above; for such recognitions and reversals will arouse either pity or fear. Now tragedy is an imitation of just such actions [as arouse pity and fear], and it is the same sort of action which will bring about good and bad fortune. Moreover, since the recognition [we are speaking of] is a recognition of certain individuals, in some cases, where, for instance, it is already evident who one of two people is, there is need of only one recognition—that which will reveal who the other person is. But sometimes the identity of both parties must be made known, as Iphigenia is recognized by Orestes from the sending of a letter, but there is need of another recognition so that he may become known to her.

The tragic   The two parts of a plot which are concerned with
experience these matters are, then, reversal and recognition. But there is a third element—the tragic experience. Reversal and recognition have been defined. The tragic experience is: destructive or painful actions such as deaths in plain view, extreme pains, wounds, and the like.

12

Technical parts   We have already mentioned the elements which must be considered as essential parts of tragedy.[13] The number

---

[13] This chapter (12) interrupts Aristotle's discussion of plot and thus seems out of place. Some doubt its authenticity, especially at this point in the discussion. The marked similarity of the first two and the last two lines of the paragraph increases the suspicion already cast upon the entire passage.

and separate parts into which a tragedy is regularly divided are: (1) prologue, (2) episode, (3) exode, and (4) choral odes which are subdivided into (a) parodus and (b) stasima. These parts are common to all tragedies, and some particular ones have in addition (5) songs from the stage and (6) commoi. The prologue is that entire part of the tragedy which precedes the entrance ode of the chorus. An episode is that entire part of the tragedy which comes between choral odes. An exode is that entire part of the tragedy after which there is no [complete] [14] choral ode. The parodus is the first complete ode of the chorus. A stasimon is a song of the chorus without anapests and trochaics.[15] A commus is an [antiphonal] lamentation between the chorus and one or more of the actors on the stage. The elements which must be considered as essential parts of tragedy were given above. These parts here listed are the number and separate parts into which tragedy is regularly divided.

13

We should next take up in our discussion (1) what it is that those who construct plots must aim at, (2) what must be avoided, and (3) by what means the [proper] function of tragedy is to be effected. Since the plot of the best type of tragedy must not be simple but complex, and since it must be an imitation of actions which arouse pity and fear—which is the peculiar function of the imitation which tragedy portrays—it is evident, first of all, that (1) good men must not be shown passing from good into evil

Aim and function of tragedy

[14] It seems advisable to add this adjective, for many Greek tragedies end with a short statement by the chorus.
[15] This may have been an adequate definition for the stasima written in Aristotle's day (fourth century B.C.), but it is not adequate for those in the fifth-century tragedies which have survived.

fortune; for that arouses neither pity nor fear, but aversion. Nor (2) must evil men be shown passing from misfortune into good fortune. That type of situation is most ill-suited to tragedy, since it has none of the essentials required of tragedy. It neither satisfies man's general sympathetic feeling for man, nor arouses pity or fear. Nor again (3) must a very wicked person be portrayed as passing from good to bad fortune; for even though such a plot would satisfy man's general sympathetic feeling for man it would not arouse pity or fear; for pity is aroused by the plight of the man who does not deserve his misfortune, and fear by the predicaments of men like ourselves.[16] Therefore, neither pity nor fear will result.[17]

The tragic character   The only type of situation left is that midway between these just mentioned. It is the situation of the man of much glory and good fortune who is not [too] superior in excellence and uprightness and yet does not come into his misfortune because of baseness and rascality but through some inadequacy or positive fault.[18] Oedipus, Thyestes,

[16] This last "for" clause is expressed twice in the Greek. Gudeman seems right in regarding the second expression of the idea as a more explicit marginal explanation which found its way into the text.

[17] I.e., from the examples just mentioned, since they are concerned neither with men like ourselves nor with a victim of undeserved misfortune.

[18] "Inadequacy or positive fault" is an attempt to render this third most difficult word (*hamartia*) in the *Poetics* to translate. The best approach to a correct understanding of what Aristotle here means by this word is to read in full chapter VIII of the 5th book of his *Nicomachean Ethics*. A part of what he there says concerning *hamartema*, which is the 3rd declension neuter equivalent of the 1st declension feminine abstract *hamartia*, is as follows: "Injuries committed in human relationships are of three kinds. (1) An injury committed in ignorance against another is a *hamartema* since the act turned out: (a) not to be what the doer supposed it would be, or (b) not to affect the person he supposed it would affect, or (c) not through the means he supposed, or (d) not with the result he supposed. For either: (a) he did not sup-

and famous men of such houses are evident examples. It
is necessary, then, for the well-arranged plot (1) to be
single rather than, as some say, double in outcome; (2)
for the change of fortune to be from good to bad but not
from bad to good; and (3) for this change to be brought
about not by rascality but by a striking inadequacy or   *hamartia*
positive fault, either in a person of the type just mentioned, or in a better rather than in an inferior person.
Experience proves that this is so; for at first tragic poets
used any stories they cared to. But now the best tragedies
center about only a few families: about such men as Alcmeon, Oedipus, Orestes, Meleager, Thyestes, Telephus,
and as many others as happened to do or experience terrible things.

According to art, then, the best tragedies are con-   *The correct*
structed along these lines. Therefore, those who blame   *ending*
Euripides because he follows this practice in his tragedies
and has many of them end unhappily are in error. As was
just said, this is the correct ending, and here is the great-

~~~~~~~~~~~~~~~~~~~~~~~~~~

pose he was striking anyone, or (b) he did not suppose he was
striking that particular person, or (c) he did not suppose he
would strike him with that means, or (d) he did not suppose
he would strike him with that result, but all turned out different
from what he supposed. . . . Whenever, then, an injury to another is caused by an act in no way expected to injure it is an
atychema. But an injury caused by an act expected to injure but
with no evil intent, as when a person really wounds another
while he intended only to prick him is a *hamartema*; for one commits a *hamartema* whenever the originating cause of the injury
is within himself, and one commits an *atychema* (misadventure)
when the originating cause of the injury is outside himself."
    Except for the meanings "guilt" and "sin," which the lexicon
limits to philosophical and religious use, the only other meanings
given in the new Liddell & Scott for this word (*hamartia*) when
it is used without qualifiers are: (1) "failure" and (2) "fault."
These two meanings, as well as the tragedies themselves, seem to
indicate that a hero's tragedy may be due (1) to an inadequacy,
or (2) to an active fault. The above translation is an effort to
include both these ideas.

est proof of it: on the stage and in the contests, such plays, if their plots are well constructed, appear to be the most tragic; and Euripides, even if he does not construct his plots well in other respects, appears to be the most tragic of the poets.

The double ending   The second type of plot is that which is ranked by some as first. It has a twofold arrangement, as the *Odyssey* does, and has a different ending for the good and the bad characters. But it is the weak character of the spectators which makes this seem the best type of plot; for the poets, as they write, follow the wishes of the spectators.[19] But the pleasure this type of plot gives is inherent in comedy but foreign to tragedy; for in comedy those who are enemies according to the plot—Orestes and Aegisthus, for instance—become friends at the end and go off stage without anyone's being killed by anybody.

14

Pity and fear through spectacle   Now it is possible for pity and fear to be aroused (1) through pageant and spectacle as well as (2) from the arrangement of the incidents. The latter is better, and is characteristic of the better poet; for the plot should be so constructed that, apart from what is taken in through the eye, anyone just listening to the incidents, as they take place, would chill with fear and thrill with pity from what is happening. Such would be the experience of one listening to the plot of the *Oedipus Tyrannus*. But to undertake to produce such an effect through pageant and spectacle is more inartistic and requires a lot of stage apparatus. And those who, while striving to achieve that which arouses fear, produce only what is monstrous, are

[19] Plato testifies to the same degeneracy in poetic standards in his protest against it in *Laws* II, 659 a-c.

total strangers to [the nature and purpose of] tragedy; for one must not expect every kind of pleasure from tragedy, but only that pleasure which is peculiar to it. Since the pleasure to be derived from pity and fear must be created by the poet through imitation of an action, it is evident that this [means for pleasure from pity and fear] must be inherent in the incidents of the action.

What, then, are the sorts of actions which seem fearful *Kinds of* and arouse pity? They must necessarily be such as happen *tragic action* between (1) friends, or (2) enemies, or (3) those who are neither. Now if the action is one of an enemy against an enemy, there is nothing, either in the act or in its intention, to arouse pity, unless it be the mere suffering.[20] The same would be true in the case of those who were neither friends nor foes. But whenever the tragic action is against a member of the family, such as when a brother either kills or intends to kill a brother, a son a father, a mother a son or a son a mother, or does some other deed of this kind, these are the materials which the tragic poet must be on the look-out for. He must not upset the traditionally accepted plots, such as having Clytemnestra killed by Orestes and Eriphyle by Alcmeon, but he must devise ways and means of using well these traditional plots. Let us make clearer what we mean by "using them well."

One arrangement is to have the deed done, as it was in early tragedies, by characters who are entirely conscious and aware of what they are doing, as Euripides has Medea kill her children, fully aware of what she is doing. A second arrangement is to have the characters do the terrible deed but do it in ignorance and later discover their rela-

---

[20] To Greek feeling, apart from the rarest noble exceptions, it was all right for a person to have his enemies, to hate them cordially, and treat them accordingly. This was considered the normal and expected thing.

tionship, as the Oedipus of Sophocles does. Oedipus' terrible deed was really outside the action of the drama, but there are cases where such deeds happen within the tragedy. The *Alcmeon* of Astydamus or Telegonus in *The Wounded Odysseus* are examples. The third choice is to have the character on the verge of doing some irreparable deed through ignorance and then discover what he is about to do before he does it.

These are the only possible choices; for one must either act or not act, and must do so either knowing or not knowing what he is doing. The poorest of these [artistically] is to have a character knowingly intend to do something and then not do it. It is abhorrent but not tragic, since no tragic deed happens. Consequently, no one acts thus in tragedy, except occasionally, as when Haemon almost kills Creon in the *Antigone*. The next choice is to have the character do the deed. It is better for him to do it in ignorance and discover [the true situation] later; for to do it in ignorance relieves it of being abhorrent, and the recognition is startling. The third and last choice is the best. I mean such as that of Merope in the *Cresphontes*, who is about to kill her son but discovers who he is before she kills him, or the sister who is about to kill her brother in the *Iphigenia*, or the son in the *Helle* who recognizes his mother just as he is about to surrender her. This is the reason, as was said earlier, why tragedies center about a few families. For it was while they were searching by chance and not through any rules of art that the poets discovered the sort of material they should have in their plots. They were then compelled to turn to such houses as had had such experiences. This is enough to say about the arrangement of the incidents and about the kind of plot tragedy must have.

15

In regard to character in tragedy, four qualities must be aimed at. The first and foremost is that it be good. A tragedy will have character if, as has been said, its language and action make clear some choice [of the speaker or doer] and the character will be good if the choice made evident is a good one. This quality of good is possible in every class of persons; for even a woman and a slave are good; yet a woman is perhaps an inferior thing while a slave is wholly inconsequential. The second quality demanded is that the character be fitting; [21] for there is such a thing as manly character, but it is not fitting for a woman to be manly or clever. The third quality required of character in tragedy is that of "likeness"; [22] for this is different from making character good and fitting as we have defined the terms.

The fourth quality is consistency. Even if the person portrayed in the imitation is inconsistent and has been given that type of character, he must be consistently inconsistent. Menelaus in the *Orestes* is an example of unnecessary baseness of character. The speech of Melanippe as well as the lament of Odysseus in the *Scylla* are examples of unbecoming and inappropriate character. An example of inconsistency in character is seen in *Iphigenia*

Prerequisites for the character of tragic characters

Good

Fitting

"Likeness"

Consistency

---

[21] By "fitting," which is listed as the second quality demanded, Aristotle *seems to mean* "befitting" the genus or class to which the portrayed character belongs—man, woman, slave, nobility, etc.; befitting the nature of each as a class.

[22] By "likeness" he *seems to mean*: likeness in character to the traditional character being portrayed. To portray an Antigone one should have not only Antigone's character *in general* but her character and characteristic reactions *in particular*. To portray Oedipus one should be not only easily given to anger *in general* but to the type of anger which is characteristic of that hero. Etc.

The necessary
or probable
aimed at

Dénouement

Incidents should
accord with
reason

at Aulis;[23] for as a suppliant in that play she seems quite a different person from what she is later on in the play.

It is also necessary in character portrayal, just as it was in arranging the incidents, to aim always at what is necessary or what is probable in such a way that when a certain type of person says or does a certain type of thing he does so either from necessity or probability; and when one thing follows another, it shall do so either from necessity or probability. It is evident, therefore, that the dénouement of a plot must result naturally from the plot itself and not from a *deus ex machina*, as in the *Medea*, nor as it happens in the return in the *Iliad*. The *deus ex machina* must be used for matters outside the drama, for antecedent elements which it is not possible for man to know, or for subsequent matters which need to be reported or foretold; for we attribute to the gods the ability to see all things.[24]

There must be nothing contrary to reason in the incidents; and if there is, it must be outside the tragedy, as the illogical element is in Sophocles' *Oedipus Tyrannus*.[25] Since tragedy is an imitation of actions of superior men, we must follow the practice of good portrait painters; for these, even though they depict men as they are in their individual physical forms, paint them better than they are. In just the same way, a poet making an imitation of men who are irascible, easy-going, or otherwise similarly disposed in their characters, must raise them, in spite of such

[23] Most editions take this to refer to the play by Euripides. But Mr. Fyfe seems to take it to mean "Iphigenia while at Aulis." The Greek is not explicit.

[24] Remember that *deus ex machina* means literally "god from a machine." It was generally a deity or near deity who was thus brought into a play.

[25] The illogicality in the Oedipus story is that he had married Jocasta and lived in Thebes with her as long as he did without finding out that she was his mother.

character traits, to a fitting nobility, as Achilles, an example of obstinacy, has been made noble by Homer.[26] These things, then, must be kept in mind by the poet, as he must also keep in mind those elements involved in seeing the play [27] which are a necessary part of the art of poetry; for it is possible to make many slips in handling these also. But such matters have been sufficiently discussed in works already published.

16

We have explained earlier what we mean by recognition. Now a word about the different kinds of recognition. *Kinds of recognition* The first, which is the most inartistic but most frequently used by the poets because of their lack of inventiveness, is recognition through signs. Of these, some are marks the *Through signs* characters are born with, such as the "spearhead which the giants carry" or the kind of stars Carcinus used in his *Thyestes*,[28] while some are acquired. Of those acquired, some are bodily marks, such as scars, and some are mere attachments to the body, such as necklaces and the ark used in the *Tyro*. But there is also a better and a worse way to use even these, as his scar made Odysseus known to the nurse in one way and to the swineherd in another. Recognition and all similar scenes merely for the sake of proof are more inartistic; but recognitions arising from a reversal, as in the *Niptroi* [*Washers*] are better.

~~~~~~~~~~~~~~~~~~

[26] I have followed Gudeman's text in the latter part of this sentence. He reads *agathon* (acc. sing. masc. of the Greek adj. "good") modifying Achilles instead of the nominative of the proper noun *Agathon*, which most texts read.

[27] I.e., stage effects.

[28] The "spearhead" and "stars" here mentioned are said to be birthmarks characteristic of certain families.

Through inven-   Second among the kinds of recognition are those [not
tions of the poet in the myth but] invented by the poet and therefore inartistic. An instance of this kind is found in the *Iphigenia,*
when Orestes makes known that he is Orestes. Iphigenia
is made known through a letter, but Orestes says not
what the myth says but what the poet wants him to say.
Therefore, we have in this play something close to the
mistake already mentioned; for Orestes could have brought
along some "signs." We have also the sound of the shuttle
in Sophocles' *Tereus.*

Through   The third kind of recognition comes about through
memory memory. In this type of recognition one is made known
through one's reaction upon seeing something, such as the
recognition scene in the *Cyprii* of Dicaeogenes, where the
character weeps when he sees a picture. Of the same type
is the scene in the tale of Alcinous,[29] when, upon hearing
a cithara player and being reminded by him, Odysseus
bursts into tears and is thereby recognized.

Through   The fourth kind is brought about through reasoning,
reasoning as in the *Choephori* where it is reasoned: some similar
person has come; there is no similar person except Orestes; therefore Orestes has come. The tragedy of Iphigenia
by Polyidus, the sophist, has an example; for it was natural
for Orestes to reason [aloud and thus be recognized] [30]
that his sister has been sacrificed and now he too is being
sacrificed. So too in the *Tydeus* of Theodectus he reasoned [and was thus recognized] that he had come to
find a son but was himself being destroyed. Such also is
the recognition in the *Phinidae;* for when the women see
the place they reason that they are fated to die there,
since it was there they were exposed.

[29] *Odyssey* 8:521.
[30] See *infra,* chapter 17, toward the end of the "generalized
sketch of the Iphigenia story," for this addition.

There is also a sort of composite recognition which re- *From false* sults from a false inference of one of the characters, as in *inferences* *Odysseus the False Messenger.* This play has Odysseus say that he will recognize a bow which he had not seen. There- fore, to portray another person as recognizing Odysseus from this statement is false reasoning.

Of all forms of recognition the best is that which re- sults from the incidents themselves in which the astonish- ment too results from what is probable. Such are the rec- ognitions in Sophocles' *Oedipus Tyrannus* and in the *Iphigenia;* for it was natural for Iphigenia to want to send a letter home. These are the only kinds of recognition which are devoid of artificial tokens such as necklaces. The second best type of recognition consists of those which are brought about by reasoning.

17

In working out the plot and in adding the language *The whole situ-* which will aid its effect, the poet should, as far as possible, *ation should be* keep the whole situation visualized before him. If he thus *visualized* visualizes it, seeing everything with the greatest clarity as if he were actually beholding it as a spectator, he should discover whatever is fitting [for the action] and at the same time discern any lurking incongruities. The scene for which Carcinus is criticized furnishes an example. By not visualizing the scene as a spectator, he failed to take account of Amphiaraüs' coming out of the temple.[31] But when the play was presented it was a failure because the spectators were displeased with this scene.

Furthermore, as far as possible, the poet should work *Gestures should* *be visualized*

[31] Gudeman's text is here followed, since it seems nearer the MSS. than Bywater's, which is here based on a seemingly gratui- tous emendation by Vahlen.

out his imitation under the [imaginative] impact of even the [proper] gestures; for, given the same ability, those are more convincing who undergo the emotional experience [being portrayed]. A distressed person communicates that feeling to others with the greatest reality. The same is true of an angry person. Therefore, the art of poetry demands either an inspired person, or a man of genius; [32] for the former is easily lifted out of himself, while the latter readily takes on various feelings and moods.

Plots should be sketched   Both traditional and invented plots should be first sketched as a general whole and then have the episodes put in and be [otherwise] filled out. A generalized sketch of the Iphigenia story as I here mean would be about like this:

A maiden, who had been sacrificed but had disappeared secretly in the process and was taken into another country in which it was customary to sacrifice strangers to the goddess [Artemis], was priestess in the temple of that goddess. At a later time her brother happened to come there, but the fact that the god told him to go there for a certain reason is outside the generalized sketch of the plot, as is also his purpose in going there. When he has arrived there, has been arrested, and is about to be sacrificed, he is recognized, either as Euripides brings it about, by having him make himself known, or as Polyidus does, by having him say quite naturally that not only was his sister sacrificed but that he too must be, and because of that remark was saved.

After this, when the names have been added, the episodes may then be put in. The poet must see to it that the epi-

---

[32] By adding the Greek word for "rather" in this sentence Gudeman gets a text which means: "poetry demands a man of genius rather than an inspired one." The idea in the Greek text as it stands is certainly a true Greek idea. See Plato's *Ion* and his *Phaedrus* 245a.

sodes are inherently related to the plot, just as is the case with Orestes' madness, through which he was arrested, and his getting away by means of the [feigned] cleansing.

In drama the episodes are brief, but epic poetry gains *Episodes brief* its length through its episodes. The story of the *Odyssey* is not a long one:

A certain man is away from home for a number of years, being closely watched by Poseidon and stripped of all his companions, while his affairs at home are in such shape that his money is being squandered by wooers of his wife, and his son is being plotted against. After being shipwrecked by a storm, he arrives home, makes himself known to some, and attacks the wooers, with the result that he is saved and his enemies destroyed.

That is the real story of the *Odyssey*. The rest is episodes.

18

Every tragedy has (1) complication and (2) dénoue- *Complication* ment. The incidents outside the drama and some of those *and dénouement* within it generally constitute the complication. The rest is dénouement. By "complication" I mean everything from the beginning of the play up to the last part of the action just before the change into good fortune (****). The dénouement consists of everything from the beginning of the change [of fortune] to the end of the play. In the *Lynceus* of Theodectus the complication consists of the events which preceded [the seizure of the boy], the seizure of the boy, and then their [33] own seizure. The dénouement is everything from the indictment for the murder to the end of the play.

[33] The Greek does not make clear who the "their" is.

Kinds of   There are four kinds of tragedy, the same in number
tragedy as the essential elements we have [thus far] discussed.[34]
There are (1) complex tragedies, those which are wholly
reversal and recognition; (2) tragedies of suffering, such
as those dealing with the Ajaxes and Ixions; (3) character
tragedies, such as the *Peleus* and *The Women of Phthiotis;*
and (4) tragedies depending upon spectacle, such as *Prometheus, The Daughters of Phorcys,* and those with
scenes laid in Hades.

It seems imperative, then, for the poet to try to include
all elements, or, if not all, he should certainly include the
most important and the greatest number of them he can,
especially since there is now so much captious criticism
of the poets. Just because there have been poets who
were, each of them, good in the use of some one of these
essential elements, people now think that one man should
surpass all the individual excellencies of previous poets.

The best criterion for deciding whether tragedies are
similar in kind or not is the plot. This is another way of
saying: decide by whether they have similar complications
and dénouements. Many poets who handle their complications well handle their dénouements poorly. But the
poet should always be master of both.

Epic plots   One should remember what has frequently been said:
unsuitable that tragedy should not employ the epic type of plot—
one with many legends [and thus plots within plots]—just
as if one should use the entire story of the *Iliad* for a tragedy. The parts [various legends] of an epic poem get

---

[34] An unclear, and apparently not very accurate, reference. Professor Cooper's translation (p. 61) has what seems the most probable explanation. Aristotle's discussion from chapters 11 through 13
has centered about: (1) reversal and discovery, (2) the tragic experience, and (3) the role of character in tragedy, with (4) some
mention of the role of spectacle. The four types of tragedy listed
in this paragraph correspond roughly with these four elements.

their proper magnitude because of the length of the poem, but in tragedy such parts produce an effect quite different from what one would expect. This is proved by the fact that those who have treated the entire story of the sack of Ilium rather than a part of it, as Euripides has, or the complete story of Niobe rather than as Aeschylus has, have either failed with their presentations or have made a poor showing in the contests. This is the one fault which caused even Agathon to fail.

In reversals and in simple plots, tragic poets are aiming admirably at what they desire, namely: what is both tragic and in accord with man's general sympathetic feeling for man. Such an aim is achieved when a clever scoundrel like Sisyphus has been deceived, or when a brave but wicked person has been defeated. This is probable, just as Agathon says; for it is probable that even many improbable things happen.

The chorus should be regarded as one of the actors, as *The chorus* a constituent part of the whole, and should share in the action as Sophocles, and not as Euripides, has it do. In the case of the other [tragic poets] the choral odes have no more connection with their plot than with some other tragedy.[35] Consequently, their choral odes have become interpolations, a practice begun by Agathon. And yet, what is the difference between using interpolated odes and taking the long messenger's speech [36] or an episode out of one play and inserting it in another?

19

Now that we have spoken of the other parts of trag- *Diction and thought*

---

[35] Aristotle must mean "the rest except Aeschylus"; for this statement is not true of the choral odes in Aeschylean drama.

[36] See *infra*, section III, note 7.

edy, it remains to speak of diction and thought.[37] In regard to thought, let us just assume what has been said on this subject in the treatise on rhetoric, since this belongs more properly to that inquiry. Under thought is subsumed all those things which must be effected by speech, such as presentation of a case, disproving a charge or ameliorating a situation, arousing the tragic elements of fear, pity, anger, and the like, and also curtailing and enlarging upon matters. It is evident that one must draw from the same principles also [as in speaking] in their actions whenever it is necessary to produce what is pitiful, fearful, great or probable, but with this difference [in mind]: action should make its purpose and effect evident without being helped by language, while the effects to be produced by speech should be achieved by the speaker and come into being as a result of his speech. For what could be the use of a speaker if matters were already as clear as they should be?

In regard to diction, one phase of the inquiry is the arrangement of words for effect. A person skilled in the art of declamation or some such master art of interpretation should be expert in this. Diction deals with such questions as: what is a question, a prayer, a statement, a threat, an answer, and other similar matters. But the poet's knowledge or ignorance of these matters has not brought against the art of poetry any criticism worthy of serious consideration. For how could anyone suppose that the criticism Protagoras leveled at Homer was really a fault—that in saying: "sing, goddess, the wrath" [of Achilles], Homer had really issued a command when he had thought he was uttering a prayer? For to bid one to do or not to do something is, he argues, a command. But let us pass over such

---

[37] Aristotle seems here to be thinking of the mind as a maneuverer of language to produce or aid certain effects.

matters since they belong to some other art than that of poetry.

20

The whole of diction consists of the following parts: [38] letters, syllables, binding words, joining words, nouns, verbs, inflection, and clauses and sentences.[39]

A "letter" is an indivisible sound from which sounds *Elements of* having signification can naturally be formed. Not all such *diction* sounds are "letters"; for there are indivisible sounds of animals, which could not be called "letters." "Letters" are of three kinds: vowels, semivowels, and mutes. A vowel is a "letter" which has an audible sound of its own without the addition of any other element. A semivowel is one which requires some additional element like an *s* or an *r* if it is to have an audible sound. A mute is one which even with an additional element still has no sound of its own but becomes audible when joined with such elements as a *g* or a *d*, which do have a sound. The ["letters"] differ: (1) in the shape and place of the mouth [they are sounded in], (2) in roughness and smoothness, (3) in length and shortness, and (4) in the pitch of voice used—high, low, or medium. But a detailed treatment of these matters belongs to a discussion of metres.

A "syllable" is a composite sound without meaning

[38] This and the following chapters (20 and 21) of the *Poetics* have a very tenuous connection with the art of poetry. The Greek must have puzzled ancient as well as modern scholars; for the text is so confused and some of the words have such a variety of meanings that one cannot always be certain what the Greek says, much less what Aristotle means.

[39] No Greek word has a greater variety of meanings than the one used here (*logos*). It may mean a single word, or any group of words thought of as a unit. Hence the double translation.

made up of a mute and some element having a sound. *Gr* without an *a* forms a syllable; and so does *gr* with an *a* [*gra*]. But an inquiry into the differences in the elements [of a syllable] belongs also to a discussion of the metrical art.

A "binding word" [48] is a sound without meaning which neither hinders nor causes the formation of a single significant sound from more sounds, and which does not fittingly stand in its own right at the beginning of a clause or sentence. Such Greek words as *men, toi, de,* etc., are examples. Or it is a sound without meaning which is able to make one significant sound out of sounds which are more in number and have significance (****).

A "joining word" is a sound without meaning which marks the beginning, end, or division of a sentence or clause, and is naturally placed at the ends or in the middle.[41]

A "noun" is a significant composite sound without temporal signification, whose component parts have no significance when taken separately; for in compound words we do not use the component parts separately in their individual signification. Thus in the noun Theodorus the significance of *doron* [gift] is not felt.

A "verb" is a significant composite sound with a time element, whose component parts have no significance when taken separately, just as was the case with nouns. The word "man" or "white" does not signify "when"; but "walks" and "has walked" signify present and past time respectively.

---

[40] Greek had, like German, many particles which, in themselves, had little meaning but were used to determine the emphasis or "turn" to be given some word, or clause, or even an entire sentence.

[41] The Greeks had fewer punctuation marks than we do. They used certain short words or particles to show certain relations which we indicate by punctuation.

"Inflection" applies to nouns and verbs, and deals with indications of: (1) [the relationships] "of this," "for this," etc.; (2) number, whether one or many, such as "men" or "man"; and (3) the manner of execution, whether it is a question or a command, for instance. For "did he go?" or "go" is an inflection of the verb in this latter aspect.

A "clause" is a significant composite sound some parts of which have a signification in and of themselves, just as the noun Cleon has in the expression "Cleon is walking." Yet not every clause is made up of verbs and nouns, as the expression "the definition of man" will make clear. It is possible to have one without a verb, but it will always contain some part which is significant. A clause is a unit in two ways: either by having a single signification in and of itself or by being linked with more [words and phrases], just as the *Iliad* is a unity from having its parts properly linked together, while the definition of man is a unity because it signifies one thing.

21

There are two kinds of nouns: simple and compound. By a "simple noun" I mean one made up of parts without meaning, as the word *ge* [earth] is. By a "compound noun" I mean one made up either (1) of parts each of which has a meaning, or (2) of a part with and a part without meaning but with the meaning and lack of meaning of the parts unapparent in the noun. It is possible to have nouns of three parts, four parts, or even many parts, like the numerous parts of grandiloquent compounds such as "Hermo-caeco-xanthus" [42] (****).

[42] "A compound of three river names: Hermus, Caicus and Xanthus, after which something seems to have been lost from the text." —Bywater's note.

Every word [noun?] [43] is either: (1) familiar or strange; (2) of transferred meanings or ornamental; (3) invented; (4) lengthened; (5) shortened; or (6) altered. I mean by a "familiar" word one which everybody uses, and by a "strange" word one which another people use. Consequently, it is evident that the same word can be both familiar and strange, but not to the same people. Thus the Cyprian word for "spear" is familiar to the Cyprians but strange to us.

A word [noun?] "of transferred meaning" [44] is one which has "inherited" another meaning either (1) from genus to species, or (2) from species to genus, or (3) from species to species, or (4) by analogy. By "from genus to species" I mean such as this: "Here *stands* my ship"; for riding at anchor is a species of *standing*. An example of "from species to genus" is: "*Ten thousand* goodly deeds has Odysseus wrought"; for ten thousand is [a species of the genus] "much" and is here used instead of "much." An example of "from species to species" is: "Having *taken away* his life with bronze," or "Having *cut* him down with unwearied bronze." In these quotations "take away" is used for "cut," and "cut" is used for "take away"; for both are "species" of "taking away."

By "transferred meaning from analogy" I mean whenever a second term is to the first as a fourth is to the third; for then the fourth can be used for the second or the second for the fourth. And sometimes that to which a

~~~~~~~~~~~~~~

[43] The Greek word used here (*onoma*) generally means, in discussions about language, "noun." But the discussion in what follows here seems to turn at times on verb forms and at times on nouns. Hence the more non-committal translation "word."

[44] The Greek word used here is *metaphora* meaning "transference, change." In discussions dealing with language it means: "transference of a word to a new sense" (new Liddell & Scott). It seems to cover the principle in language which we call metonyme, as will be clear from what follows.

person is closely related is used for the person. Thus if a cup is to Dionysus as a shield is to Ares, one may call a cup a "shield of Dionysus" and a shield "the cup of Ares." Or if old age is to life what evening is to day, one may speak of evening as "the old age of day" or as Empedocles spoke of it,[45] and of old age as the "evening of life" or the "sunset of life."

But there is no word corresponding to some of the "transferred meanings by analogy," yet the principle is applied none the less. For instance, to scatter seed-grain is called "sowing," but there is no word to denote the [similar action of] the sun as it scatters its flame. Yet this scattering of its flame is to the sun as sowing is to seed-grain. Therefore, men speak of "sowing the god-created flame." It is possible by this practice to use this transference of meaning in still another way: by adding a foreign meaning but at the same time denying to the word some of the significations belonging to its new meaning; thus one might call a shield not the "cup of Ares" but a "wineless cup." (****).

An "invented word" is one which is not in use at all but has been coined by the poet himself. There seem to be some words of this kind. "Sprouters" for *horns* and "pray-er" for *priest* are examples.

A word is "lengthened" if it uses a longer vowel than it naturally should, or if a syllable has been added; and it is "shortened" if any part of it is taken away. *Polēos* [46] for *poleos* and *Pelēïadeō* for *Peleidou* are examples of length-

<hr>

[45] What Empedocles said is not known. Gudeman brackets this clause as insufficiently authenticated.

[46] The Greeks had different letters for long and short *e*, as they did also for long and short *o*. Hence these two forms, which are spelled with the same letters in English, would be spelled with different letters in Greek. Then, too, certain preceding short vowels could be contracted with certain succeeding vowels.

ened words. Examples of shortened ones are *kri* [for *krithe*] *do* [for *doma*] and *ops* [for *opis*] in expressions such as "becomes one *ops* [view] of both." [47]

A word is said to be "altered" whenever a part of it has been left [as it was] and an invented part added. Thus we find *dexiteron* instead of *dexion* [in *Iliad* 5:393].

Of nouns themselves, some are masculine, some feminine, and some are neuter gender. Those ending in *nu* [n], *rho* [r], *sigma* [s] and in the two compounds of sigma[s], *psi* and *ksi*, are masculine. Those ending in the two vowels which are always long, eta [ē] and *omega* [ō], and those ending in *alpha* [a], which is one of the vowels that may be lengthened, are feminine. Thus it turns out that the number of endings for masculine and feminine nouns is the same, since *psi* and *ksi* are the same as sigma [s]. There are no nouns ending in a mute or a short vowel. Only three end in *iota* [i]: *meli* [honey], *kommi* [gum] and *peperi* [pepper]. Five end in *upsilon* [u].[48] Neuter nouns end in these letters [*upsilon?* and *iota?*] and in *nu* [n] and *sigma* [s].

~~~~~~~~~~~~~~~~

[47] The words within the quotation marks are merely a literal rendering of a fragment attributed to Empedocles. See Diels, *Fragments of the Presocratics (Fragmente der Vorsokratiker)* B 88 under Empedocles. It is impossible to tell from these four words, extracted as they are from their context, just what the expression means or refers to.

[48] The general straining for consistency in Gudeman's text is well illustrated here. The text merely says: "five end in *upsilon.*" But Gudeman lists in brackets in his text five Greek neuter nouns which do end in *upsilon*, and cites as his first and only early "authority" for them the lost fifth- or sixth-century (A.D.) manuscript which he claims was the basis for the lost Syriac translation which is believed to be the basis for the extant Arabic version.

Gudeman then finds himself put to it to dispose of the nine additional Greek neuter nouns in *upsilon* listed by Herodian. The argument he uses would dispose summarily of two of the three in *iota* which the standard text lists as given by Aristotle.

22

The function of diction is (1) to make clear what is *Function of* said and (2) to lift it above the level of the ordinary. A *diction* diction which uses familiar words is the clearest, but it is also ordinary. This is illustrated by the poetry of Cleophon and Sthenelus. Diction becomes stately and removed from the common idiom by using foreign words. And I mean by "foreign words": (1) rare words, (2) words with transferred meanings, (3) lengthened words, and (4) everything which is opposite to the ordinary. Yet if one should go too far in these matters the result will be either jargon or riddles. An excessive use of words with transferred meanings [tends to] produce riddles and an excessive use of rare words produces jargon; for the essence of riddling is to unite in a sentence things which cannot be united—and this cannot be done by uniting regular ordinary words but only by using those with transferred meanings—such as "I saw a man by fire weld bronze upon a man," [49] and similar expressions.

Jargon results from the use of rare words. Therefore, a *Importance of* writer must somehow get a [proper] mixture of rare *correct diction* words and of those with transferred meanings; for a mixture of rare words, of words with transferred meanings, of ornamental words, and of the other kinds already mentioned will lend a tone of professional skill and elevation to the diction, while the familiar words will make for clarity. The lengthening, shortening, and altering of words contributes most to clarity of diction and to expression which is above the ordinary; for it will produce something above the ordinary on account of its

[49] A riddle based upon the "operation" known as cupping with a cupping glass.

being different from the familiar and the customary, and it will be clear on account of its having something in common with the ordinary. Therefore, those critics are wrong who censure this kind of diction and satirize the poets, as the elder Euclides did, on the ground that it is easy to write poetry, provided one is allowed to lengthen his words as much as he wishes. He caricatured [this practice] in this very diction by reading as verses of poetry:

"I saw Epichares strolling towards Marathon," and
"He (?) couldn't enamored as he was, of this man's hellebore." [50]

An obvious striving after a style like this is ridiculous. Moderation must characterize all parts [of diction]; for one could produce the same effect by using words of transferred meanings, or rare words, or by using other kinds of words improperly for the purpose of raising a laugh.

How much difference the use of fitting words makes in epic poetry may be seen by substituting ordinary words in the verses. Anyone can see the truth of what we are saying if he will substitute in epic poetry familiar nouns for the rare ones, for those with transferred meanings, and for the other kinds. For instance, both Aeschylus and

~~~~~~~~~~~~~~~~~~~~

[50] It is impossible to translate these lines in such a way as to make Aristotle's full meaning clear. Greek metres were determined by long and short syllables and not by stress accent. Euclides is here simply stringing Greek words together without any regard for whether or not words and syllables with long and short vowels come in those places where the metre demands that they come. In other words, "These two quotations are given as specimens of prose which by a liberal use of epic licences may be made to read as verse." (Bywater's note.) The text of the second of these quotations is hopelessly corrupt. Translators (except Margoliouth, who uses a different text) refuse to translate it. The present translation is hardly more than a guess which has been ventured for the purpose of making this translation of the *Poetics* a complete one.

Euripides wrote an iambic line which was identical except for just one word, a rare word instead of a familiar one, with the result that one seems beautiful and the other ordinary. Aeschylus in his *Philoctetes* wrote: "An ulcerous cancer which eats the flesh of this my foot." Instead of "eats" Euripides used in his line "feasts upon." So too the line [51] "Now this weak pigmy wretch, of mean design" if anyone should substitute familiar words, would read: "Now just a little, ugly weakling" has blinded me.

[*Odyssey* 20:259 reads]: "He places for him 'a trivet-table and ignobler seat'" [Pope]. With familiar words it would read: "He brought in a broken-down stool and a little old table for him."

Thus, too, "the shores resound" becomes "the shores scream out." And yet Ariphrades used to satirize the tragic poets for using words and expressions which could not be used in ordinary speech, such as "from home away" [he went] instead of [he went] "away from home"; or such [archaic] Greek expressions as *sethen* [for *sou*] and *ego de nin;* or [whenever they say] "Achilles concerning" instead of "concerning Achilles," and use other such expressions. The fact that all such expressions are not made up of ordinary words gives an uncommon flavor to the diction. But Ariphrades was not aware of this.

It is important to use compound words, rare words, and every element of diction properly. But to make sure that words of transferred meanings are properly used is by far the most important; for this is the one thing which cannot be learned from others. It is a sure sign of inborn talent; for one must have a good eye for similarities if one is to use nouns of transferred meanings well. Compound words are especially fitting for the dithyramb, rare words

[51] Homer's *Odyssey* 9:515 (Pope's translation).

for heroic poetry, and words with transferred meanings for iambic poetry. In heroic poetry all the kinds of words mentioned are useful, but in iambic poetry, since it, more than any other form of poetry, aims to imitate ordinary speech, those words which would be used in prose are most fitting. These [prose words] are (1) ordinary words, (2) words with transferred meanings, and (3) ornamental words. And so, as regards tragedy and imitation in action let these things which have been said be considered sufficient.

III

EPIC POETRY

23

Now about the art of poetry through narration and   *Plot in epic* through imitation in metre only [i.e., epic poetry]. It is evident that it must have a plot, just as tragedy does, dramatically constructed about a single action which is whole and complete, with a beginning, a middle, and an end. This is necessary so that it, as a united whole, may impart its peculiar pleasure as living organisms do. The arrangement of an epic must be different from that of histories,[1] in which the problem is not to make evident the parts of a single action but to set forth those events of a single period of time which centered about one or about several persons but were only incidentally related to each other. For instance, the battle of Salamis and the Carthaginian battle in Sicily happened at the same time but they did not converge towards the same end. In just the same way events sometimes merely follow each other in successive points of time without tending towards an end. Yet

---

[1] Gudeman's text is here followed, since it seemed certainly as near the MSS. and decidedly less forced than Bywater's.

practically all the poets do this.[2] Therefore, as we have already said, in this, too, the divine Homer would appear superior to other writers; for even though the Trojan war had a beginning and an end, he did not try to use the whole of it in his poem. Its magnitude would have been too great and it would not have been easy to comprehend as a whole; or, if he had modified its magnitude, it would have been complicated by the variety of its events. But, in actual fact, it was one part of the war that Homer chose and varied his poem at intervals by the use of many episodes such as the catalogue of ships, etc. Other writers center their poems about one individual, or about one time or one action of many parts, as the author of the *Cypria* and *The Little Iliad* has done. Therefore, not more than one tragedy, or at most two, is based on the *Iliad*. The same is true of the *Odyssey*. But there are many from the *Cypria* and more than eight from *The Little Iliad*: for instance, *The Contest for the Arms, Philoctetes, Neoptolemus, Eurypylus, The Begging, Laconian Women, The Sack of Ilium, The Sailings, Sinon*, and *The Trojan Women.*

24

Kinds of epic   There must be the same kinds of epic poetry as there are tragedies: (1) simple epics, (2) complex epics, (3) epics based on suffering, and (4) epics based on ethical choices. Except for music and spectacle, the parts are the same; for epics too must have reversals, recognitions, tragic experiences, character [indicants], and good diction. Homer employs all these, and he was the first to use them and use them as they should be: for he wrote one

---

[2] I.e., arrange their material as though they were writing history instead of epic.

of his poems, the *Iliad*, as a simple poem based on suffering; and the other, the *Odyssey*, as a complex work, full of recognitions and based on ethical choices. In addition to these virtues, his poems surpass all others in diction and in thought.

Yet epic poetry differs [from tragedy] both in the *Length* length of the composition and in metre. The limit already laid down for the length is sufficient, i.e., a length which can be comprehended from beginning to end simultaneously as a whole.[3] Such would be the case if the ancient epics were shorter and approached [in length] the tragedies presented at one hearing.[4] The fact that it is impossible to represent simultaneously in tragedy several parts of the action, but only those which are being presented on the stage through the actors, means that epic poetry has a very distinct advantage for extending its length a good deal. For the fact that epic poetry is narrative makes it possible to present many parts [of the story] as happening at the same time. If these parts are germane to the sub-

[3] *Supra,* p. 16.

[4] The meaning of this sentence is not as clear as it may at first seem. (1) Does he mean to include in his "ancient epics" the *Iliad* and the *Odyssey,* or is he referring to ancient epics other than these two which he so often singles out for praise? All other extant ancient epics are much shorter than the two Homeric poems.

(2) Does he mean by "tragedies" the trilogy or the tetralogy which each competing poet had to present?

(3) Does he mean by "presented at one hearing" just the tetralogy presented each morning of the festival, or is he here using the phrase to include all the nine or twelve tragedies presented during the entire "single" festival, as Fyfe argues?

It seems simpler to interpret the sentence as Professor Cooper does: to mean that the required time-limit laid down by Aristotle would be feasible for epic (Homer and all the others) if its length should be made about the same as that of a trilogy or a tetralogy, i.e., about 4000 lines or a little beyond that. The Oxford text of the *Iliad* now has 15,680 lines and the same text of the *Odyssey* has 12,109.

ject the bulk of the poem will be increased. This has the advantage (1) of giving grandeur to the poem, (2) of affording a change for the listener, and (3) of diversifying the poem with dissimilar episodes; for sameness quickly surfeits an audience and causes tragedies to fail.

Metre   The fitting metre for heroic poetry was arrived at through experience; and if an imitation through narration should be attempted in any other or in several metres the result would be something unbefitting epic poetry; for the heroic metre has the steadiest firmness and the most rounded fulness of all metres. It therefore most readily admits [into its rhythm] rare words and words with transferred meanings. Narrative imitation goes beyond the other types (****). The iambic and the trochaic tetrameter are the metres of movement, the trochaic for dancing and the iambic for dramatic action. Something still more unnatural results when anyone mixes these metres as Chaeremon has. And so, no one has ever written a long composition in any metre except in the heroic, and, as we have said, it was nature herself which taught poets the fitting metre for such.

The poet's part   Homer deserves praise for many other reasons but particularly because he alone of the poets saw clearly what he was to do. He saw that the poet himself should speak very little, since he is not an imitator if he uses that method. Other poets assume an active role throughout the whole of their poems. They seldom imitate, and even then not very much. But Homer, after a few lines of introduction, immediately brings in a man or woman or some other character—never a characterless person but one with [definite] characteristics.

Best epic material   That which produces wonder and surprise is suitable for tragedy, but the unaccountable, which is the greatest source of wonder, is more suitable for epic poetry. This is due to the fact that the actors of an epic poem are not *seen*. The pursuit of Hector on the stage, with the army standing instead of pursuing and Achilles nodding to them to leave Hector for him to slay,[5] would be ridiculous. But in epic poetry such details are not noticed. That which excites wonder and surprise is pleasant to people, as may be seen from the fact that everyone, when relating [such incidents] makes additions because he thinks they are pleasing.

Homer, more than any other poet, has taught others how what is untrue should be presented, i.e., in such a way as to produce false reasoning. Whenever one thing is portrayed as existing or happening because a former thing exists or happens, men tend to believe that if the latter is true, the first must exist or happen. But this is not true. Therefore, if the antecedent to a thing does not exist and the thing itself can exist or happen only if the antecedent does exist, the poet must center on presenting the thing itself; for our assurance of the fact that the thing itself is true makes our minds falsely infer that the antecedent is also true. There is an example of this in *The Washers*. *Presentation of the untrue*

Poets should choose impossibilities which are probable rather than possibilities which are unconvincing. They should not make their plots from parts which are contrary to reason. The best thing is for a plot to have no part which is at variance with reason. If it does, such an element should lie outside the part of the story being presented, like Oedipus' not knowing how Laius died, and not within the drama, like the description of the Pythian games in the *Electra*,[6] or the person in the *Mysians* who *Probable impossibilities versus unconvincing possibilities*

---

[5] As in *Iliad* 22:136-230.
[6] The passage is anachronistic, and such passages seem to have been offensive to Aristotle.

went from Tegea to Mysia without speaking. To say that this would ruin the story is ridiculous. Such stories should never be written, in the first place, but when they have been, and seem to admit of a treatment more in accord with reason, their absurdity becomes clear. If those parts of the *Odyssey* at variance with reason—those about Odysseus' being disembarked from a ship without being wakened—should be written by an inferior poet, it would at once be evident how intolerable they are. But Homer covers up these absurd parts with his poetic charm and other virtues.

The fullest use of diction must be made in the "idle" parts,[7] and not in those which portray character or display thought; for a very brilliant diction obscures both character [indicants] and the part played by the [character's] thought.

[7] I.e., such as the long descriptive passages one finds in Homer. *Iliad* 1:254-282 and *Odyssey* 7:80-133 are examples. Fyfe seems wrong in taking Aristotle to refer here to those long, rapid descriptions by messengers found generally near the end of Greek tragedies. They are technically called *rheses* (plu.) or *rhesis* (sing.).

IV

CRITICISMS OF POETRY

25

[Literary critical] problems and their solutions, as well *Limitations* as the number and the kinds of forms they rise from, *upon a poet* would become clear if viewed in this way: (1) Since a poet is just as much of an imitator as a painter or any other kind of creator of objective images, he must always make his imitation in one of the three possible ways: as the objects were or are, as they seem or are said to be, or as they should be. (2) A poet's imitation is achieved by means of a [plain] diction or one with rare words and words of transferred meanings.[1] Diction has many moods and feelings, all of which are allowed to poets. (3) And besides all this, the standard for correctness is not the same for the political art or for any other art and the art of poetry.

Two kinds of mistakes occur in the art of poetry: one *Kinds of mis-* a mistake in the art itself, and the other an error in inci- *takes in poetry*

---

[1] This seems to be the meaning of Bywater's text. Gudeman's is smoother and less ambiguous. His text has "in which" instead of "or," and reads ". . . through a diction in which there are rare words and words of transferred meanings."

dental matters. If a person decides to make an imitation (****), his mistakes will be in matters pertaining to the art itself.[2] But if he decides to make his imitation in the wrong way, like portraying a horse as bringing forward both his right feet at the same time or some slip such as one might make in the art of medicine or any other of the arts, or if he has employed incidents of any sort which cannot be true, then his mistake will not be in matters pertaining to the art itself. Consequently, the criticisms leveled at poetry in these [critical] problems must be answered in the light of the premises here laid down.

Answers to criticisms   Let us take up first criticisms brought against the art of poetry itself. "A poem consisting of incidents which cannot be true has been written and a mistake has been made." But the mistake is permissible if the end of poetry, which has already been stated, is thereby attained, through thus making either that part itself or some other part of the poem more striking. The pursuit of Hector [3] furnishes an example. But if it was possible to obtain the object of the poem either better or as well without departing from the rules of art governing these matters, then the mistake is not a justifiable one; for there should be no mistake at all in a poem, whenever that is possible. Moreover, it should be asked what sort of a mistake has been made—one in a matter of poetic art or an incidental one in some other field; for not to know that a hind has no horns is not as serious a mistake as to portray a deer contrary to the laws of art.

Moreover, if the objection is raised: "This is not true," the answer is: "Perhaps the poet is portraying it *as it*

---

[2] The lacuna at this point in the text makes any certain and clear meaning of the sentence impossible. Those interested further may consult Bywater's note on this line.

[3] See *supra,* p. 53.

should be," as Sophocles said he portrayed men as they should be while Euripides portrayed them as they were. If the poet has neither of these in mind,[4] one might answer: "This is the way men say it is," much as they say, though no one knows, about matters pertaining to the gods. Perhaps these statements give neither a better nor a true version of these matters but are just what Xenophanes thought they were—mere tales. But they at least accord with *what men say*. A third answer might be: "Perhaps the poet has not portrayed this as it should be but as it is [and it only seems untrue]," like Homer's statement about the spears: "Their spears stood upright with their butt-spikes in the ground."[5] This was the custom in Homer's time as it still is among the Illyrians.

In determining whether something said or done by a person is proper or not, one must look not only at the thing done or said to see whether it is good or bad, but also at the person acting or speaking, noting: (1) at whom the act or remark is directed, (2) when, (3) for whom, and (4) for the sake of what, whether to obtain a greater good, for instance, or to avoid a greater evil.

Criticisms directed at diction [6] may be answered on the basis of whether or not the expression contains a rare word. For instance, Homer says: "The shafts of the gods *Diction as a source of mis-understanding*

---

[4] I.e., whether he is portraying men as better or as they are.

[5] *Iliad* 10:152.

[6] The rest of this chapter (25) can hardly be made intelligible by translation because Greek words are under discussion. The criticisms and answers taken up turn on (1) whether we still have the word the poet really used, (2) whether the critic is giving the word the same accent the poet gave it (the difference in Greek words is often just a difference in accent), and (3) whether the poet gave the word a rare meaning or a different meaning it had taken on. Those interested in a fuller meaning of this section should consult Bywater's notes and Mr. Fyfe's translation and notes in the Loeb Library series.

fell first upon the mules." [7] But perhaps Homer did not use the word to mean "mules," but "guards." Again he says of Dolon: "Indeed, in form he was no goodly person." [8] Homer may not have been referring to any lack of bodily symmetry but to his ugly face; for even now among the Cretans a person who has merely a beautiful face is said to be a person of beautiful form. Still again, when Homer says: "Mix the wine livelier," [9] he may not be calling for undiluted wine such as drunkards demand but may simply mean "Pour it faster."

Moreover, there are criticisms to be answered on the basis of words of transferred meanings. For instance, Homer says: "Then all the other gods and men slept (****) all night long." [10] He says, too: "When indeed he gazed upon the Trojan plain, of 'flutes' and Panpipes (****)." [11] In the first quotation he uses "all" for "many"; for all is a species of the genus many. So too in the expression "alone without a share," [12] we have a case of transferred meaning. He calls the *best known one* the *only one*.

Accent There are criticisms which vanish with a change of accent, just as Hippias of Thasos changed [by merely changing the accent]: "we give to him" to the imperative "give to him." [13] By a similar means he changed also:

~~~~~~~~~~~~~~~~~~~

[7] *Iliad* 1:50. The word used for mules is a poetic word and is actually used in *Iliad* 10:84, through confusion with a somewhat similar word, to mean "guards."

[8] *Iliad* 10:316. The word here translated "not goodly" means also "ugly."

[9] *Iliad* 9:203.

[10] *Iliad* 2:1.

[11] *Iliad* 10:11. On the word "flute" see *supra*, section 1, note 2.

[12] *Iliad* 18:489.

[13] This expression is too short and too common to be located definitely. It is generally referred to *Iliad* 21:297, or to an early reading of *Iliad* 2:15.

"which is not rotted by the rain" to "a part of which is rotted by the rain." [14] Then, too, some criticisms vanish with a change of "punctuation," as in the statement of Empedocles: "Straightway there came forth mortal ele- *Punctuation* ments which until then had learned immortal things and pure formerly were mingled." [15] Still others are due to ambiguity. This is the case in: "The night has gone for- *Ambiguity* ward more." [16] The word for "more" is ambiguous.

And still others have arisen from certain customary *Extended cus-* expressions. Men mix water with wine but still call the *tomary expres-* mixture wine. This furnishes an analogue for such poetic *sions* expressions as: "Greaves of new-wrought tin." [17] Men also call workers in iron "bronze-smiths," which furnishes an analogy for Ganymede's being said "to pour wine for the gods," even though the gods do not drink wine.[18] This could be explained also on the basis of words of transferred meanings.

Whenever a word seems to have an opposite meaning [from what it should], one should also consider in how many ways it could have this meaning in the expression in which it occurs. For instance, in the clause: "[the gold layer] in which was checked [Aeneas'] brazen spear," [19] one should consider in how many ways it is possible for

---

[14] *Iliad* 23:327.

[15] Diels, Frag. 35, 14-15. One punctuation makes "formerly" modify "pure"; another makes it go with the verb.

[16] *Iliad* 10:252. The word here translated "more" is ambiguous because it is similar in spelling to some forms of the Greek adjective "full."

[17] *Iliad* 21:592. Tin is the most important element in bronze, the metal used by the Greeks in making greaves. Hence it is possible to speak of "greaves of tin" on the same basis that one speaks of a mixture of water and wine as wine.

[18] For the formula by which this explanation is arrived at, see *supra,* p. 42, paragraph 3. Fyfe's note is: "Nectar : gods :: wine : men. Therefore, . . . nectar may be called 'wine' or 'wine of the gods.' "

[19] *Iliad* 20:272.

spears to be checked by gold, viewing it in this way and that, but above everything else assuming all the while an attitude which is just the opposite from that mentioned by Glaucon. He says that critics first assume some un-*Presuppositions* reasoned presuppositions and proceed to discuss a poem *in readers* with their minds already made up; and then, as though the poet had said what they think he did, these men proceed to criticize the poem, if it runs counter to their own [preconceived] notions. This is the way the facts about Icarius have been treated. He was assumed to be a Spartan, and it was thought strange that Telamachus did not find Icarius when Telemachus went to Sparta in search of him.[20] But the facts may be as the Cephallenians say they are—that Odysseus married a Cephallenian whose father's name was not Icarius but Icadius. And so it is likely that the problem arose from a mistake.

Criticism con-   Generally speaking, criticisms of the impossible in *cerning the* poetry should be answered on the basis of: (1) the ideal, *impossible* (2) popular opinion, and (3) the demands of poetry. For poetry, a convincing impossibility is preferable to an unconvincing possibility. (****) [it may be impossible for] such men to exist as Zeuxis paints, but it is better [that he so portray them]; for one should surpass one's model.

Criticism con-   Elements contrary to reason may be defended by say-*cerning the* ing: "That's the way men *say* they are." One might add *unreasonable* also that such elements are not always contrary to reason; for it is probable that things do happen contrary to probability.

Criticism con-   Statements [interpreted] as contradictory should be ex-*cerning the* amined in the same way that refutations in discussions are: *contradictory* to see whether, in the light of what the poet [actually] says or what a sensible person would suppose he says,

[20] *Odyssey* 4.

these interpreters have in mind the same thing [the poet did] and have in mind the same referents and in the same manner.

Criticism of what is contrary to reason and of depravity is entirely proper, whenever such elements are not necessary and no [good] use is made of them, as is true of the irrational element in Euripides' *Aegeus* and of the depravity of Orestes in his *Menelaus*.

There are, then, five kinds of criticisms of poetry—that it contains elements which are either (1) impossible, (2) contrary to reason, (3) harmful, (4) contradictory, or (5) contrary to artistic correctness. The answers to these criticisms must be sought along the lines of the twelve answers and approaches we have suggested.

V

EPIC AND TRAGEDY
COMPARED

26

One could raise the question as to which is the higher type of imitation, epic or tragedy. If the less vulgar is higher and is always addressed to a better audience, then that which [like tragedy], is addressed to everybody is quite evidently vulgar; for actors, assuming that the audience never understands unless a great deal is added to the imitation, add a great amount of bodily action, like bad "flute" players who wind themselves around and around when they have to imitate quoits-hurlers, or grab the leader of the chorus and hustle him around whenever they are playing Scylla. This, then, is the way people think of *Actors* tragedy,[1] which is just the way earlier actors regarded their successors. Mynniscus used to call Callippides a "monkey" because of his excessive overacting. Pindar had a similar reputation. The whole art [of tragedy] is to epic poetry as these later actors were to the former. Epic poetry is said to be addressed to cultured hearers who

[1] I.e., as more ordinary and plebeian than epic.

have no need of "aids to understanding," while tragedy is addressed to ordinary people. If, then, it is vulgar, it must evidently be inferior.

Now this is not, in the first place, so much an accusation against the art of poetry as it is against the art of acting; for it is perfectly possible for a reciter of epic poetry to overdo his gestures, as Sosistratus did. The same is true of singing, as Mnasitheus the Opuntian proves. And besides, not all gestures should be rejected, any more than all dancing should, but only those of bad actors. This is what Callippides was criticized for, and modern actors are censured too because they imitate "women who are not ladies" [Fyfe]. Remember, too, that tragedy can achieve its effect without gestures from actors just as well as an epic can. Its quality becomes evident even when it is read. If, then, tragedy is shown to be superior in all other respects, this [exaggeration on the part of actors] does not have to be an inherent part of it.

[Tragedy is superior], in the second place, because it has all the elements epic poetry has. It can even use the dactylic hexameter, and has in addition no small amount of music and spectacle through which its inherent pleasure is made most vivid. Then, too, it has vividness both when it is read and when it is acted. *Tragedy has all essentials of epic*

Furthermore, tragedy accomplishes its end "with greater economy of length" [Fyfe]. What is more compact is more pleasant than that which is long drawn out. Suppose, for instance, that Sophocles' *Oedipus Tyrannus* should be drawn out to the length of the *Iliad!* *Length*

Moreover, an epic imitation is less of a unity than a tragedy, as is shown by the fact that any epic furnishes material for several tragedies. Moreover, if epic poets ever do use a single plot, the resulting poem seems truncated if they treat it briefly, or if they treat it with epic fulness, *Unity* it seems too thin and watered down. I am referring in these remarks to epics which are made up of a "plurality of actions" [Bywater], as the *Iliad* and the *Odyssey* are, yet each with an appropriate magnitude. And yet the composition of these poems is the best possible, and each is an imitation of a single action as far as that is possible [in an epic poem]. If, then, tragedy is superior to epic in all these respects and also in accomplishing its artistic purpose—for tragedy must not produce just any kind of pleasure but that which has been explained [2]—it is evidently superior to epic poetry since it achieves its purpose better.

Such, then, is our discussion of tragedy and epic poetry —of these types of poetry as such, their forms and parts, the number of parts and how they differ, what contributes to success and what causes failure in writing such poems, the criticisms brought against them, and the answers to be given (****).[3]

---

[2] See *supra*, pp. 23-24 and 26-27.
[3] Compare the very first sentence of the *Poetics.*

FOR FURTHER STUDY CONCERN-
ING THE *POETICS*

If interested in texts, translations, articles, etc., concerning the
Poetics, consult Cooper and Gudeman's *A Bibliography of the
Poetics of Aristotle*, Yale University Press (1928). This volume
lists 1,583 items. To this should be added:

Gudeman's text with notes and apparatus (1934);

Gilbert's translation (see Preface, p. ix) based on this new text
by Gudeman; and

W. Hamilton Fyfe's *Aristotle's Art of Poetry*, Oxford University Press (1940).

The two most widely recognized texts and translations of the
Poetics are:

S. H. Butcher's *Aristotle's Theory of Poetry and Fine Art*
4th ed., MacMillan Co. (1911), and

Ingram Bywater's *Aristotle on the Art of Poetry*, Oxford at
the Clarendon Press (1909).

If interested in the manuscript evidence for the *Poetics*, begin
with E. Lobel's *The Greek Manuscripts of Aristotle's Poetics*
(1933) in Vol. IX of the Supplement to the Biographical Society's
Transactions.

An outline of the matters discussed in the *Poetics* can be most
quickly seen:

(1) in the Table of Contents to Butcher's translation,

(2) from the sectional headings throughout Gilbert's translation,

(3) from the chapter headings in Fyfe's translation (see above),

(4) from the marginal outline in Mr. Lane Cooper's translation, or

(5) from the marginal outline of the present translation.

A fuller outline may be found in A. S. Owen's companion to Bywater's translation, *An Analytic Commentary and Notes*, Oxford
at the Clarendon Press (1931).

LITERARY WORKS

REFERRED TO

IN THE *POETICS*

Aegeus, 61
Alcmeon, 28
Antheus, 19
Antigone, 28

Begging, The, 50

Centaur, 3
Choephori, 32
Contest for the Arms, 50
Cresphontes, 28
Cyclops, 4
Cypria, 50
Cyprii, 32

Daughters of Phorcys, 36
Deliad, 4

Electra, 53
Eurypylus, 50

Helle, 28

Iliad, 7, 18, 30, 36, 41, 50, 51, 63, 64
Iphigenia, 28, 32, 33
Iphigenia at Aulis, 29

Laconian Women, 50
Little Iliad, 50
Lynceus, 21, 35

Margites, 7

Medea, 30
Menelaus, 61
Mysians, 53

Neoptolemus, 50
Niptroi (Washers), 31, 53

Odysseus, The False Messenger, 33
Odyssey, 7, 17, 18, 26, 35, 50, 51, 54, 64
Oedipus (Tyrannus), 21, 26, 30, 33, 63
Orestes, 29

Peleus, 36
Philoctetes, 47, 50
Phinidae, The, 32
Prometheus, 36

Sack of Ilium, 50
Sailings, The, 50
Scylla, 29
Sinon, 50

Tereus, 32
Thyestes, 31
Trojan Women, 50
Tydeus, 32
Tyro, 31

Women of Phthiotis, 36
Wounded Odysseus, The, 28

PROPER NAMES

IN THE *POETICS*

Achilles, 31, 47, 53
Aegisthus, 26
Aeschylus, 8, 37, 46, 47
Agathon, 19, 37
Ajaxes, 36
Alcibiades, 19
Alcinous, 32
Alcmeon, 25, 27
Amphiaraüs, 33
Ares, 43
Argos, 20
Ariphrades, 47
Aristophanes, 4
Astydamus, 28
Athenians, 5
Athens, 9

Callipides, 62, 63
Carcinus, 31, 33
Cephallenians, 60
Chaeremon, 3, 52
Chionides, 5
Cleon, 41
Cleophon, 4, 45
Clytemnaestra, 27
Crates, 9
Creon, 28
Cretans, 58
Cyprians, 42

Danaus, 21
Dicaeogenes, 32
Dionysius, 3

Dionysus, 43
Dolon, 58
Dorians, 5

Empedocles, 2, 3, 43, 59
Epichares, 46
Epicharmus, 5, 9
Eriphyle, 27
Eucleides, 46
Euripides, 25, 26, 27, 34, 37, 47, 57, 61

Ganymede, 59
Glaucon, 60

Hades, 36
Haemon, 28
Hector, 53, 56
Hegemon of Thasos, 4
Heracles, 17
Herodotus, 18
Hippias of Thasos, 58
Homer, 2, 3, 4, 6, 7, 17, 18, 31, 38, 50, 52, 53, 54, 57, 58

Icadius, 60
Icarius, 60
Ilium, 37
Illyrians, 57
Iphigenia, 22, 32, 33, 34
Ixions, 36

Laius, 53

Magnes, 5
Marathon, 46
Medea, 27
Megara, 5
Megarians, 5
Melanippe, 29
Meleager, 25
Menelaus, 29
Merope, 28
Mitys, 20
Mnasitheus the Opuntian, 63
Mynniscus, 62
Mysia, 54

Nicochares, 4
Niobe, 37

Odysseus, 17, 29, 31, 32, 33, 42, 53, 54, 60
Oedipus, 21, 24, 25, 28, 53
Orestes, 22, 25, 26, 27, 32, 35, 61

Parnassus, 17
Pauson, 3
Peloponnesians, 5
Philoxenus, 4
Phormis, 9
Pindar (actor), 62

Polygnotus, 3, 14
Polyidus, 32, 34
Poseidon, 35
Protagoras, 38

Salamis, 49
Scylla, 62
Sicily, 5, 9, 49
Sisyphus, 37
Sophocles, 4, 8, 28, 30, 32, 33, 37, 57, 63
Sophron, 2
Sosistratus, 63
Sparta, 60
Sthenelus, 45

Tegea, 54
Telegonus, 28
Telemachus, 60
Telephus, 25
Theodectus, 32, 35
Theodorus, 40
Thyestes, 24, 25
Timotheus, 4

Xenarchus, 2
Xenophanes, 57
Zeuxis, 14, 60